Patterns and Designs
from the Twenties
in Full Color

Ad. and M. P. Verneuil

DOVER PUBLICATIONS, INC.
New York

Published in Canada by General Publishing Company, Ltd., 30 Lesmill
Road, Don Mills, Toronto, Ontario.
Published in the United Kingdom by Constable and Company, Ltd., 3 The
Lanchesters, 162–164 Fulham Palace Road, London W6 9ER.

This Dover edition, first published in 1993, contains, in a new layout, all 20
plates originally published in the portfolio *Kaléidoscope: ornements abstraits*,
Éditions Albert Lévy, Paris, n.d.

DOVER *Pictorial Archive* SERIES

International Standard Book Number: 0-486-27690-2

Manufactured in the United States of America
Dover Publications, Inc., 31 East 2nd Street, Mineola, N.Y. 11501

Publisher's Note

This volume reproduces, in full color, all the material from the original 20 plates (featuring 87 different patterns) in Ad. and M[aurice] P[illard] Verneuil's portfolio *Kaléidoscope: ornements abstraits*, first published by Éditions Albert Lévy in Paris sometime in the 1920s. The portfolio contained abstract patterns oriented to a great variety of design applications, including textiles, wallpaper and stencils. The forms offered included borders and allover patterns.

The complete portfolio is an artistic and technical tour de force. The reproduction method used was the pochoir process, a hand-coloring stencil technique (executed for *Kaléidoscope* by J. Saudé) employed to make many of the great design, fashion and architectural albums of the Art Nouveau and Art Deco periods. Artists and craftspeople will find the designs suitable for projects of all kinds, and art enthusiasts will return to these pages again and again, simply for another appreciative glance.

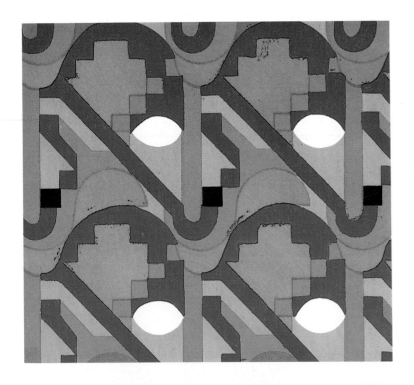

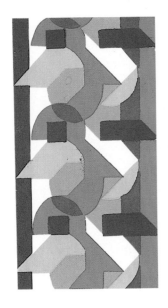

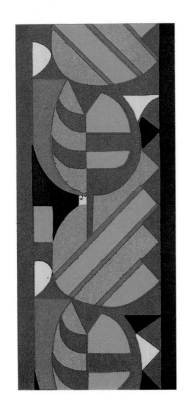

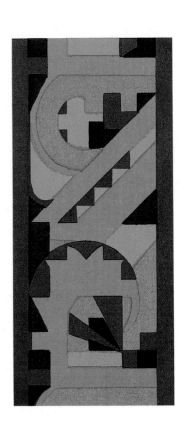

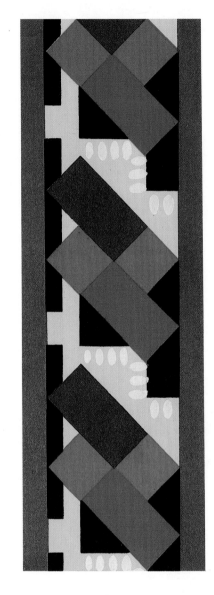

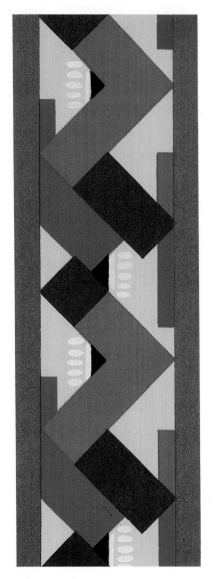

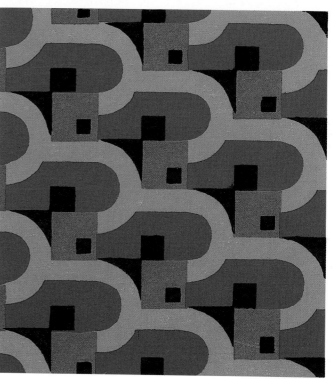